MW01225919

Lucky Thursday

Story by Trish Lawrence

Illustrations by Mark Wilson

If you go out with Ky tell Darren where you'll be.
Mum

THOMSON

™

NELSON

PM Extras Chapter Books in Emerald Level Set A

Dolphin Dreaming
Fish for Dinner
Grand Street Theatre Robbery
Lucky Thursday
Midnight in the Tunnel
Trash and Treasure

PM Extras Chapter Books
Emerald Level Set A

The PM Library is published by Thomson Learning Australia and is distributed as follows:

AUSTRALIA
102 Dodds Street
Southbank 3006
Victoria

NEW ZEALAND
Nelson Price Milburn
1 Te Puni Street
Petone

First published in 2004
10 9 8 7 6 5 4 3 2 1
07 06 05 04

Text © Nelson Australia Pty Limited 2004
Illustrations © Nelson Australia Pty Limited 2004

Lucky Thursday
    ISBN 0 17 011428 7
    ISBN 0 17 011427 9 (set)

Illustrations by Mark Wilson
Edited by Angelique Campbell-Muir
Designed by Leigh Ashforth
Typeset in Plantin
Printed in China by Midas Printing (Asia) Ltd

Nelson Australia Pty Limited ACN 058 280 149 (incorporated in Victoria)
trading as Thomson Learning Australia.

Contents

CHAPTER 1

Torrential Rain

Thursday was one of the luckiest days of my life. It was even luckier for my best friend, Ky.

My older brother, Darren, said that I shouldn't get any credit for what happened on Thursday, and he can't believe that I went where I did in the first place. But I'll let you make up your own mind.

It had started raining at about three o'clock on Wednesday. It was torrential rain. By Thursday afternoon it was still raining, and we'd got drenched coming home from school. I was on my bike and so was Ky. Miss Lang had let our class out a few minutes early when she saw the greeny black sky surging towards us from the coast.

It only took about two minutes for Ky and me to get completely saturated. Cars had pulled over by the side of the road with their lights flashing. People were huddled together under shop awnings. We rode along the footpath, glad that there were no people there to get in our way. It felt exciting and adventurous to be braving it against the elements.

As I rounded the corner I noticed that Mum's car wasn't home. Inside, Darren's bedroom door was closed and I could hear the music blasting from the other side of the walls.

It didn't take me long to find the leftover mudcake for afternoon tea and Mum's note next to it. It said that if I went out to play with Ky then I should tell Darren where I would be.

If you go out
with Ky tell
Darren where
you'll be. Mum.

First, I stripped off my wet clothes in the laundry. My school uniform left big puddles on the floor. With dry clothes on, I headed back for the mudcake. That's when the phone rang. Before I even got the receiver to my ear, Ky's voice came racing out at me.

CHAPTER 2

Down the Reserve

'There's a flood down the reserve,' said Ky. 'I'm going down for a look. Are you coming?'

I looked out of the kitchen window. The rain had finally stopped and a very hazy sun was trying to break through the clouds.

'Yeah, sure,' I said to Ky.

I shoved the rest of the cake into my mouth, grabbed my hat and raced towards the kitchen door. It was then that Mum's note blew off the counter. Remembering what Mum had said, I went back, bursting into Darren's bedroom.

What a sight!

One hundred and seventy centimetres of scrawny sixteen-year-old manhood playing air guitar in front of his mirror. But I didn't have long to laugh. A very smelly soccer boot was aimed directly at my face. I was out of there! I scrawled on the back of Mum's note: *Gone down the reserve with Ky.*

Then I left.

Ky was waiting for me at the corner of my street. We yelled with excitement, pedalling furiously as we flew down the road on our bikes. The whole street had a new, fresh smell. The heavy rain had gathered all the leaves and debris and was pushing it along towards the drains. The footpath was left clean and sparkling, tiny specks in the cement glinting in the late afternoon sun.

We couldn't have guessed what was in store for us.

Rounding the corner of the last house before the reserve, the roaring sound became almost deafening. It didn't take us long to realise what it was. All the leaves and rubbish had banked up at the drain. It had been a while since the last heavy rain, and there was stuff coming from everywhere.

Ky dropped his bike where he stood and started splashing around in the water. He tore off his T-shirt and did a belly flop into the water. Before I followed him, I pushed my bike to a higher piece of ground where it would be safe. I didn't want anything to happen to it.

CHAPTER 3

Drain Danger

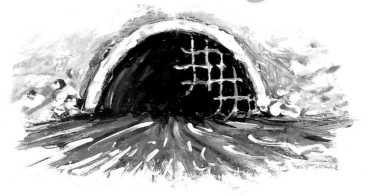

It had been fun swimming against the pull of the water as it rushed down towards the drain.

'I'm going to move some of the rubbish,' Ky shouted to me as he grabbed at a large branch with newspaper caught on it. I knew it was a bad idea, but just as I opened my mouth to tell him that he'd better stay away from the drain, it happened.

As soon as Ky moved the branch a great, gurgling tidal wave surged towards the drain.

'Jake! Help!' Ky cried out to me as the water pulled him away. 'Help! Jake, help!'

I looked around for help but there was no one else there.

Ky was hanging on to a broken piece of the metal grate. Most of it had broken off, and I wasn't sure how long this last bit would hold.

'Do something,' Ky gasped. 'Get—' Then the water gushed over him.

'Help! Help! Please – somebody – help!' I yelled, but there wasn't anyone there to hear me. I looked all around then noticed that the house on the corner had a car in the driveway. I hoped desperately that someone there might hear me.

I struggled to hold myself up against the force of the water and moved as fast as I could to the high ground behind the drain. But, by the time I'd circled around, most of Ky's body was gone. He had been swept into the drain. Only his head and his arms were still above water.

'I can't hold on much longer,' Ky said, his voice desperate.

I grabbed Ky under his arms and pulled with all my might. My muscles ached but I wouldn't stop.

'After three,' I ordered him. 'One, two, three... Now pull yourself up,' I shouted. But he didn't move at all. He looked really scared, and it shocked me.

CHAPTER 4

The Pull of the Water

Ky couldn't answer me. The muddy water swirled around his mouth, and he swallowed a mouthful. It was all I could do to pull his head clear so he could breathe.

Only Ky's eyes told the true story. He looked terrified. As I held his head up, I kept yelling for help. I tried to reassure Ky that someone would find us soon. I really hoped someone would.

I could feel the pull of the water, sucking Ky further in. I thought my arms would break trying to hold onto him. I wondered how long I could hold him. Then I saw the car start up in the driveway of the corner house.

'Over here!' I shouted 'We're over here!' I yelled as loud as I could, but I didn't dare let go to wave.

The car backed out and stopped. I thought that the driver had heard me, or even seen us. But after a minute the engine revved and the car crept slowly down the road. My chest hurt and I felt sick in the stomach.

The sun went behind a cloud and it suddenly became darker. I felt like giving up. I looked around and realised that the trees of the reserve were shading us. We wouldn't be visible to anyone from the road.

Ky's head started to flop around in the water. Every now and then, water gushed over his mouth. His hair was covering his eyes and I couldn't see if he was still conscious.

'Don't you give up!' I screamed at him. 'Don't you dare!'

I knew that I didn't have the strength to pull Ky out of that drain. Either the water had to stop running or someone had to come along and help to pull him out. But I knew that I would never let go. With my body aching all over, I secured my grip. I wasn't going anywhere.

CHAPTER 5

Waiting for Help

I don't know how long I'd been there. I saw the car from the corner house come back. I tried to yell out, but my voice was only a squeak.

Then my mind started drifting. I wondered what would be happening at my place. Was Darren still playing air guitar in his room? Would Mum be home yet?

Then I thought I saw something move at the end of the street, but it was getting darker now so I couldn't be sure. I forced myself to focus on the movement.

It looked like two people running across the reserve. One was tall and thin and was leading the way. The other one was shorter and was wearing a coat. I hoped with all my heart that they were running towards us. They stopped near the bikes and looked around. Would they think to look for us at the drain?

The next thing I knew, a beam of torchlight hit me in the face.

'Mum, they're over here!' It was Darren's voice. It was so good to hear my big brother.

CHAPTER 6

The Rescue

Mum and Darren grabbed on to Ky and we all pulled him out of the drain. Laying on his side, Ky started coughing and then shivering.

Darren picked him up in his arms like a baby. With one arm around my shoulders, and half lifting me to help me walk, Mum talked to Ky all the way back to his house. Luckily, it was nearby.

Ky's mum started screaming when she saw us coming. We got Ky inside and warmed him up. After a while Ky stopped shaking. We sat on the lounge together, with hot drinks in our hands and rugs around us. I had never felt so tired in my life.

'It's just as well you left a note, Jake,' said Darren. 'We didn't know where to look for you, but then we found the note. It had fallen on to the floor.'

'We thought you'd know better than to play in a drain,' Mum added. 'That is the last place we would have looked.'

'I'm really glad that your note said where we were,' murmured Ky, his voice still weak.

I smiled. I was glad that I had written that note as I'd dashed out. Those few seconds could have meant the difference between being rescued or not.

I suppose Darren was right about me not deserving any credit, though. After all, I was only doing what I had been told. But there was something we all agreed on – it really was a lucky Thursday.